T0095244

ALSO BY JOSEPH DORAZIO

No Small Effort

As Is: New & Selected Poems

Remains to Be Seen

Poems of the Fifth Sun

CALENDARIUM
& OTHER POEMS

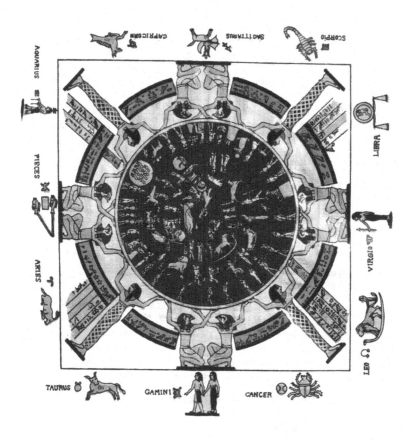

JOSEPH DORAZIO

 www.trafford.com

North America & international
toll-free: 1 888 232 4444 (USA & Canada)
fax: 812 355 4082

for Daniel

Table of Contents

Grateful acknowledgment is made to the following publications
in which these poems first appeared:

Brain of Forgetting
Chantwood Magazine
Emerge Literary Journal
Foliate Oak Literary Magazine
The Fourth River
Fredericksburg Literary & Art Review
The Magnolia Review
The Muse: An International Journal of Poetry
New Plains Review
The Poetry Porch
Symmetry Pebbles Magazine
THAT Literary Review
The Worcester Review
West Texas Literary Review
Writer's Bloc Literary Magazine
Yellow Chair Review

CALENDARIUM

Ah, we compute the years and divide them here and there and stop and begin and hesitate between both. But how of one piece is everything we encounter, how related one thing is to the next, how it gives birth to itself and grows up and is educated in its own nature, and all we basically have to do is to be, but simply, earnestly, the way the earth simply is, and gives its consent to the seasons, bright and dark and whole in space, not asking to rest upon anything other than the net of influences and forces in which the stars feel secure.

Rainer Maria Rilke, Letters on Cezanne

JANUARY

Winter's reliquary. Tinsel
ornamental reburied.
Claus more hirsute,
you resolute. Long month,
light short and ghosted;
to do's and W2s posted.
Mindset a southern hemisphere—
it's summer there, like
the thermometer you're going
nowhere anytime soon.
Open the door to a new year,
peer out—fog; slog through it
to the end, beyond dreary,
you're greeted by another month
that ends in uary.

FEBRUARY

Do the math—month number two,
years in multiples of four
get a day tacked on, and
one in four Tuesdays grows fat.
Reduce a single Wednesday to ash.
Still, all bets are off—
it's anyone's guess
when the doldrums will end
despite the groundhog's prognostications.
The month that requires a leap of faith
to suppose the sun will transcend
Cupid's miscalculations.

MARCH

Month of wishful thinking—
the passage from lion to lamb will be peaceful,
and rebirth the next sequel
in the here-we-go-again parade.
Such is the nature of round things.
Take the Earth, for example:
Europeans who once thought
the world was flat, discovered
an island they dubbed Easter,
which was someone else's home
—they didn't know that either.

3

APRIL

When daffodils burst in committee
and showers develop in spades,
the command of Aprillis to open
viburnum,
    cherry blossom,
        and tulip
over days the diamond reigns.
The first of three months with pretty maids' names
babbling no cruel decay
to all of us gullible fools.

MAY

A whiff of lilac serves
as well as any veneer
masking the base metal of the year
upon which we erect our maypoles.
The bonfires of Beltane glow,
brightening Maia's furbelows.
There's much to celebrate.
      And while
the recent charnel season
is the furthest thing from your mind,
it only demonstrates how thoroughly
this merry month called May
perfumes decay.

JUNE

Even the June bug shall have his say,
so too shall the wood thrush
despite the land's ventriloquism.
So much of what has already been said
seeks to obfuscate. Once again
the solstice returns,
its generous hours elucidate.
Perhaps too ardently we contemplate
peony as well as honeysuckle
—summer's ephemeral lessons—
only to graduate.

JULY

Found poem from a farmers almanac

The spring lambs are already sold.
The randy bull is pulled.
Suckler farmers now gauge their herds,
dose their weanlings for worm and hoose,
maintain leafy swards.
It's time to assess the winter silage:
by any reckoning there's less fodder than the year before,
and the months ahead—
no broader.

AUGUST

The garden appears deserted—
feeders aren't doing much trade.
Paris is abandoned, save for a few
poppies and glads in bloom.
It is to this lull
that we assign the adjective,
then set sail upon summer waves
on our hunt for lasting grandeur—
little Captain Ahabs
anxiously eyeing the whale spume.

SEPTEMBER

Something in the hills is
stirring. Snake skin?
Desiccated cicadas?
Something yellow. Something
in the hills has pulled the fire alarm.
Summer practice drill?
Chlorophyll crisis—code yellow.
No doubt other shades will follow in increasing timbre.
Something in my head
seeks to clarify. Thoughts—
what kind of thoughts? Ineffable,
really, try fragile favrile glass, maybe cooler Druid;
antiquey colors—hues mostly
orange or red simulated, de-escalated to pastel.
Can you say synesthesia awareness month?
Didn't want to go there. School.
Back to.
Yellow bus labors up the hill.

OCTOBER

Month of carved
gourds, ribbed
rinds aglow, guts dumped
unceremoniously on the composter.
More leaves, more mead, more
carving of daylight hours
which only seems to devour the days
between this month and the next
when all this chiseling
turns its attention
toward the bird.

NOVEMBER

The yard looks like a room
closed up for winter. Scarecrows
are wearing dead leaves.
A stingy sun can barely spare a dime,
though there's little to spend it on—
October's buskers having flown town.
Now it all comes down to the bone
structure of the landscape; down
to the cellar—a daddy longlegs' atelier
with its plein air paintings on display:
      a black buckle shoe here,
           an unfinished portrait of a Wampanoag chief
          there.

DECEMBER

No cardboard skeletons
gleefully dance the Charleston now.
No pumpkins grimace. No
cackling witches stir the heated broth—
just winter's rife frost
and Saint Nick's alchemical tricks:
earth turned to iron, water to stone.
The sobriety of another year's end
with its concentric loneliness.
The sun stands still at solstice
while the distant songs of carolers
move past in Doppler Effect
leaving you standing alone
in the silent night
suspended—

           like Lot's wife.

POEMS

We are the world's author as well as its plaything!

Jim Holt, Why Does the World Exist?

A THIN TIME OF YEAR

A razor,
the glazer,
lacquer veneer,
the month of October,
the insincere—
all congruous with
a thin time of year,
but what not to expect:
a broad brimmed
hat, a well-fed cat,
a rife August, a
coming together of all of us.
A while that intimates this:
the thinnest lamina
separates life from
the abyss.

for David & Michael

SHAKER FURNITURE

One senses
the pine and cherry
consenting
to their conversion,
petitioning the god of utility,
and the maple succumbing.
How a drawer's wooden pulls
yield to each hand, simple
not rough—rococo rebuffed.
A turned post bench or chair
plainly suited for the human form to settle
and wait for the second coming.

ODE ON A GRUEBY VASE

Whose verdant hands plucked this gourd
       To furbish in froth and verdigris?
Its buds are ready to spring forth,
       Ah, contented daffodils that repose
In faience—bliss! A vessel such as this
       Let no cucumber dare reproach
Nor gardener contest; 'twas the potter's wheel
       That spun this textured rind, this
Kaolin dream, and gave rise to imitations
       Of nature's art and William Grueby's green.

19

PURPLE

I am a pansy that grows where
no wavelength contains me
between red and blue
in distant mountains of ambiguity.
Like orange, I am possessed by no rhyme.
I am wine, and yet, the cure
for the inebriate: I am amethyst.
I am Caesar's toga, the Pope's robes,
and Prince's rain. I am not the same
as violet. I am the blood of a thousand mollusks shed
to dye Odysseus's wedding bed.
I am the essence of extravagance.
I can't be had for a song.
Nature rarer uses Yellow—Emily was wrong.
Come plumb my depths.

for Elisabeth

MILK

As if we ever had anything to cry over
prefixed to our mamma's tit
from the beginning
grass fed and all of it
bilked from the land of honey
and not because Hera spilt some
while suckling her boy her man
in a galaxy oriented this way or that
it's just a matter of fat or a percentage of
blood as in Harvey's
which we rightfully cried over.

ARCHAIC CARTON OF OATMEAL

after Rilke's Archaic Torso of Apollo

Though you'll never press close
To his salubrious chest
Nor feel the embrace of his capable arms,
His smile and sanguine jowls still cajole you;

Otherwise his great black hat could not
Stir you so, could not make morning
Glow hot past some mysterious bog
Where cranberries flare; otherwise

This Quaker would seem decapitated
Inside your constipated house—would
Not be warmed by your stories of oats

Wild and sensually sown; for here
There is not one grain that does not taste you.
You must simplify your life.

22

PET ROCK

After love has run its gamut,
walked your heart,
shorn of the obedience you seldom discuss
not to mention collar-worn,
you settle for something less hirsute and fetched.
Something more indurate.
This one's quieter, for sure,
and non-reciprocate—no strings attached.
Come to think of it, your new companion
is a more accurate reflection. Funny
how you both sit and stare at one another—
solid, stolid.

for Carmen

THE BOY WHO CRIED WOLF MARRIES RED RIDING HOOD

I saw your grandmother at the market today,
he tells her repeatedly.
I asked her to come for supper.
Don't be silly, says Red,
you know very well grandmother's been gone for years.
This goes on for some time.
The years pass.
They grow old and fat together.
There's a knock at the door.

SECOND GLANCE AT PURPLE

Purple is the most
introverted of the colors
not of the spectrum like the others,
but born from a marriage of red and blue.
Like Pluto, recently demoted,
the hues never really voted
to let purple into their inner circle.
Poets generally
avoid purple for lack of rhymes,
save curple—
Scottish slang for buttocks.

FAIRY TALE

He tried to recall a time when the workshop
hadn't mattered. When

the thrum of its motors hadn't lulled him to sleep.
His life was good, though deep down

he knew the machine did everything best.
He kept his part of the bargain:

gearwheels oiled, pistons polished,
augers and lathe kept sharp.

He held in his palm a heart-shaped plumb bob
no longer attached to its string:

this way is best, Pinocchio said to himself,
to be a real boy is just make-believe.

THEORY OF RELATIVITY

I have seen the wound that matter makes in space
Hyam Plutzik

You are a victim of time and space!
was the exhortation my father swore
he heard in the middle of the night
waking him from his drunken stupor,
the favorite ghost story he liked to tell—
how the grim voice couldn't have come
from the radio or tv, since growing up
we couldn't afford much beyond the basic
necessities, yet somehow my father
always had money for whiskey.
                              Still,
we're no closer than Parmenides was
in answering the big questions like
why time's arrow flies in only one direction
affording no chance of revisiting childhood
making it less inscrutable, or what space is made of
beyond expanding dark and mysterious matter,
or even the nature of human consciousness;
                              and how
a family's cycle of dysfunction
is but another carapace in an infinite tower of turtles,
                              so for me,
the issue isn't really whether or not I believe in God,
but who it was years ago—
who uttered those words,
filling my father with the truth.

A QUESTION FOR ENTOMOLOGISTS & PHILOSOPHERS
-OR-
ON THE SWEETNESS OF BEING

Do ants know, massed in their pheromonal frenzy
on a globe of ice cream
that has fallen in the sand and away
from the lips of Eden's insatiable hunger,
how small and vulnerable they are?
Could they comprehend how,
in the prevailing world of shores
and grains of sand—no bigger than themselves—
emotions ride like rollercoasters,
how the zenith of anticipation is followed
by the collapse that comes whenever something candied
escapes the grasp of our mandibles
falling to rest at last in the earth among the ants?
Is matter infinitely divisible, or endlessly large?
Or does there come a point in time
when we say enough!—
even one utopia is already too sweet.

A MIND OF WINTER

after Wallace Stevens

Desirous of shape and form are thoughts—
as is snow—
when they take place after the fact
as in fox tracks or likenesses of men;
once set
these effigies depict in past tense
the mind projecting winter
from the center of its own flurries.

IGLOO

Houses can be built
out of what we want
to keep out. Molded
into bricks, snow
is perfectly suitable
for insulating against
snow. Clever trick that
extreme northerners know.
Minds can be construed
in a similar fashion;
biased thoughts can stack
in a way as to preclude
what we perceive others lack.

THE MOOSE

It stepped from the forest, primordial,
and into the fertile minds of
Lucas, seven, and Erin, eight:
a moose in the road on the way to the cabin,
igniting imaginations larger than itself.
(Dad, at first uncertain
thinking it a horse loosed from its corral,
slowed his car.) An unlikely totem,
a harbinger, this moose
will inspire creative crayon renderings,
self-portraits featuring spindly legs,
ungainly sprouting bodies—
nascent beings emerging
from a past marked by abuse.
Their present: an immense love from adoptive parents,
with an enormous future yet to unfold,
lives and children of their own.
They'll recall this chance and magical encounter
with the moose, and learn its name
is from an Algonquian word meaning,
he strips off bark,
like the stripping off of childhood,
outgrown far too soon.

for Dan, Kyle, Erin, and Lucas

THE VULTURE

A bare-headed sort above ground,
nearer the clouds, he gracefully
soars in circles. On landing
he's a different bird:
the stork's doppelganger,
an awkward sideways hop,
wings raised as pyramids on either side,
hideously bald and lappet-faced,
red wattle, dips his head in and out
like a pen in an inkwell.
The mortician of Memphis,
he's content to leave the eyes to crows,
tail to a jackal. He peels from the anus,
bearded disembowler,
gorges on putrefied innards
until his crop is carrion-stuffed.
Praise Nekhbet. Praise
Pharaoh, whose rarified liver
was never gobbled like this.

BUNGLED

Intent on making a fly,
God began to multi-task
and set to work on man.
But things went awry. Man
was supposed to get the wings
and the compound eyes, but
got instead an intellect—
a proboscis he inserts
in regurgitated matter
while the fly vomits bliss
and dies within an hour.

CASPER'S LAW

*Casper's Law of decomposition states that a body
left in the open air decomposes twice as fast as if
it were immersed in water and eight times faster
than if it were buried underground.*

Consider how the writhing beetle, sacred scarab,
dispatched by ants—consumed
becomes the colony, or the Buddhist monk
defleshed and to the vultures tossed
rests scattered in the firmament. But
the mummified—formaldehyde infused
and casketed—aren't food for anybody;
delaying Casper's Law they lie in state
in palls resurrected by floods
washed up on someone's lawn.

34

RED HERRING

All too willing to give chase, we
dash off headlong, shout follow me!
Each day heralds new pursuits,
unleashed hounds and riding boots;

it matters not what sort of quarry,
the commonest being good green money;
the hunt itself is seldom questioned,
entitlements ordained, ourselves destined;

no sooner is the fox cornered, trapped,
we seek another trophy to distract
us from the marrow we're loathe to face:
what's really going on here in the first place.

MURDER MYSTERY IN MONOCHROME

The theater is showing red
tonight as crowds coagulate
under a sanguinary sky. A
cardinal cries his metallic what-cheer,
what-cheer, what-cheer.

She doesn't remember a time
in the cinematic past when
pictures were green or blue,
back then, in a world less vermilion,
what folks saw—they didn't do.

She's seated in the front row
wearing a garnet dress; a poppy
corsage adorns her breast.
When the moment arrives,
that dreadful moment in the movie

when the gigantic Bolshevik
is murdered in cold crimson,
without a clue you may have guessed,
she sheds a single tear
in that singular hue.

WRONGFUL DEATH

The family says they'll sue for wrongful death.
Last night I watched a nature
program where a crocodile lunged from the river
clamping its snout down on a zebra's haunches—
sheered its entire rear quarters off in one bite,
Nile bowel red with black & white.
Definitely negligence on the croc's part.
The halved zebra came to rest on the bank:
enter the vultures, jackals, and hyenas—
gold-digging lawyers come to press their case.
Here, take my card.
Family says they want compensation,
the jackals—full bellies.
Survival begets misconduct.
But couldn't Mulungu, creator of all things,
have made it so that basilisks need not claw & tear at carcasses—
ruthless dog-eat-dog vicious?
Why not a world less ravenous, less toothed
where every wildebeest finally lies gently down?
I don't know.
I only read about a wrongful death suit—
as if
any demise
in this fallen paradise
                is rightful.

DISPOSSESSED

He longed to sink into the abyss, into
the indigoes of the Marianas Trench, alive

in the realization of its bona fide depths
or to drift out among the quasars at night

that he might delight in their philosophy of distances.
He wanted to know his own marrow—

how it would feel—the full heft of the earth
upon his bones, magma thickening his thin world;

only then could he be freed from superficiality—
from fake friends

but since, like them, he sprang from the human shoal—
from the same shallow spectacle—

he can only imagine what it would be like
to have a soul.

THE MAGNIFICENT CAUSE OF BEING

after Wallace Stevens

The world is as we imagine it to be.
From our châteaus, we arrange the cosmos
as if arranging furniture—a mountain
here or there, a settee beside a window.
Our observations conjure a universe:
a hornet rests on a harp, a girl
strums a chord on her blue guitar—
alluding to the instability of emptiness.
The lucent sun, itself conceived,
finds us inside our homes; we are there
still by night dreaming
while a clock on the wall ticktocks time's motif.
Paradoxically, the only thing we cannot perceive
is our own magnificent imagination,
so we invent a deity
and insist that this deity has to be—
an inexplicable certainty.

39

Not "Revelation"—'tis—that waits,
But our unfurnished eyes—

Emily Dickinson

JOSEPH DORAZIO's poems have appeared nationally and internationally in over sixty literary venues. Winner of the 8th Annual Charlotte Miller Simon Poetry Award and BCTV's Poets Pause poetry contest, Dorazio's poems have been anthologized and set to music.

Printed in the United States
By Bookmasters